Mental Health
Therapy journal prompts

Myself:

Benefits of journal prompt for therapy:

1. Helps You Relax

One of the most significant benefits of writing journal entries is the fact that it assists you in relaxing. Writing can ease anxiety in your head.

Writing things down will not only make you feel more at ease, but you'll gain a new view of the problems you have to deal with.

In just a few moments every day to write down what you think about, you will practically instantly improve your mental and physical well-being.

2. Keep Connected to Your Emotions

Many people, especially children, have a difficult time and find it difficult to express their feelings. This could affect your mental well-being.

Writing can be an excellent method of staying conscious of your emotions. With prompts from a therapy journal such as this one, you'll be able to remain in touch with your feelings and pinpoint the reasons for stressors.

Journaling is a recent study that has revealed that journaling can help improve mental health issues.

3. Enhance Your Mood and Increase and Boost Your Creativity

One of the significant positive mental health effects of journaling is improved spirit and creativity. For people who struggle to write down their thoughts, you can draw them.

Journaling helps you think about your experiences in the past and your current state of mind.

When you recognize the things that cause you to feel upset, you can make choices that prevent these feelings from returning. Journal writing is a safe place for you to vent your feelings.

The prompts for your therapy journal below will prompt you to ask tough questions that will prompt you to reflect on your present state of mind and challenge the negative thoughts you're currently experiencing.

Date:

Write down your thoughts now. What is the first thought you think of?

_____
_____
_____
_____
_____
_____
_____
_____
_____
_____
_____
_____
_____
_____
_____

Date:

Think of the initial emotions that you're feeling at the moment?

Date:

What is the most positive emotion you're experiencing currently?

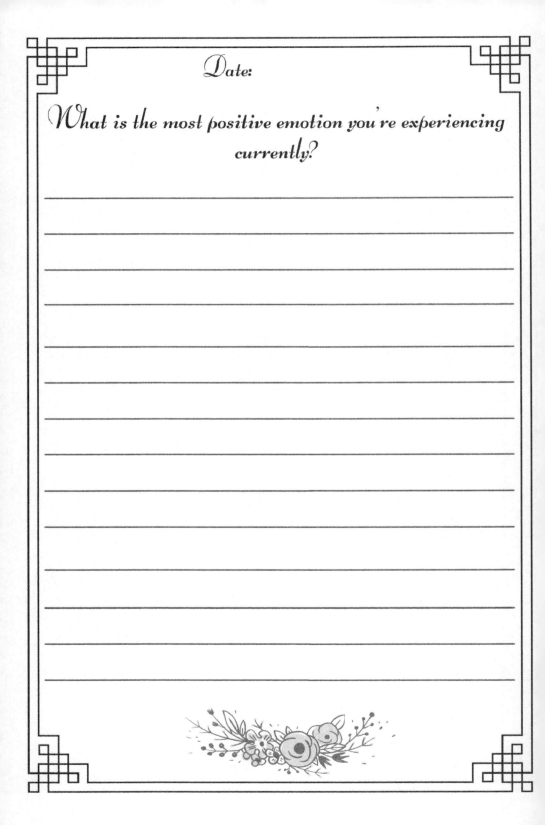

Date:

Do you recall that first moment you felt lonely?

Date:

Write down the ten items that have made you feel good today.

_____
_____
_____
_____
_____
_____
_____
_____
_____
_____
_____
_____
_____
_____
_____
_____
_____

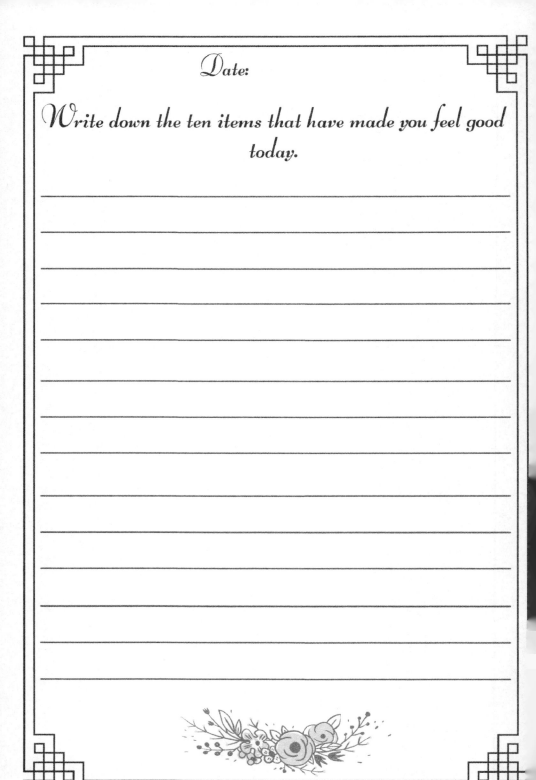

Date:

Write down two things that stress you out this morning?

___

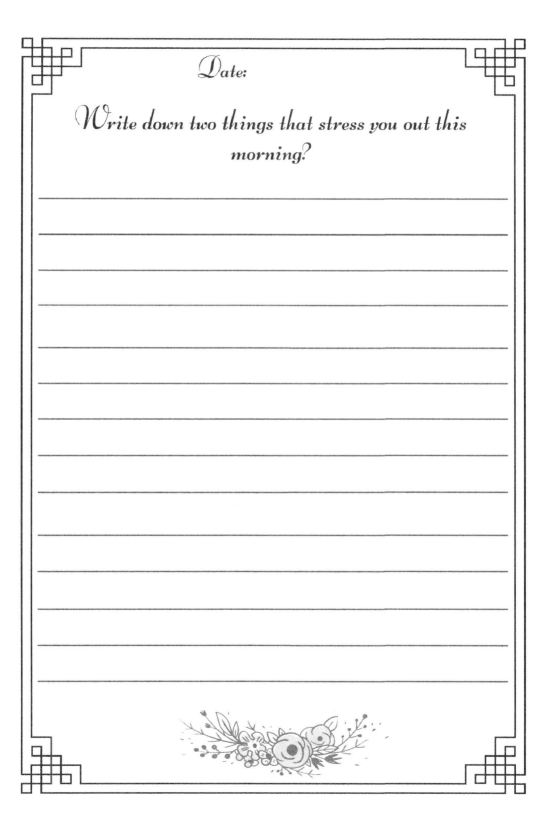

Date:

Name those you'd phone when you're nervous?

Date:

Does being on your own make you feel anxious?

Date:

Write down the five things you need to stop doing to feel more confident about yourself?

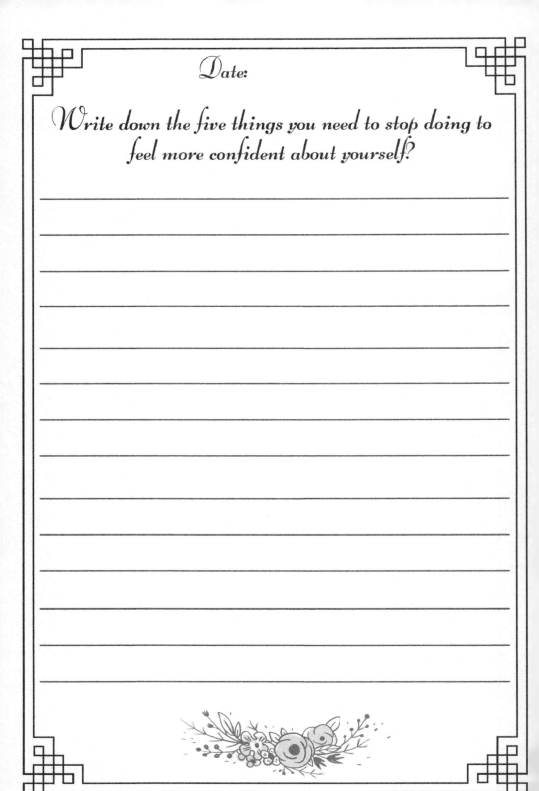

Date:

Write the two things you feel cause you to feel anxious?

_____
_____
_____
_____
_____
_____
_____
_____
_____
_____
_____
_____
_____
_____
_____

Date:

Do you believe that you've got a reliable support system that can help you deal with the challenges you're experiencing at the moment?

Date:

If you could only pick something stresses have taught you,, what is it?

Date:

From all the struggles you've had to face, What is the most important thing you learned away that strengthened you?

_____
_____
_____
_____
_____
_____
_____
_____
_____
_____
_____
_____
_____
_____
_____
_____
_____

Date:

What are the signs you can use to suggest that you're being anxious?

___
___
___
___
___
___
___
___
___
___
___
___
___
___

Date:

Are all anxiety types the same?

$\mathcal{D}$ate:

Write down your triggers for anxiety?

$\mathcal{D}$ate:

$\mathcal{W}$rite down the ten things you're thankful for in your life.

Date:

Write an open letter of love to yourself

Date:

What has made you smile today?

Date:

Write an apology letter to yourself. What are the things you're willing to do you want to forgive yourself for?

Date:

Write your list of television shows you'd like to watch when you're feeling down

Date:

If you were everywhere in the universe today, what would you like to be?

Date:

Write down your list of activities you could do when stressed. For instance, you could take a deep breath, go on long walks or read a book, enjoy a cup of coffee with a companion etc.

_____
_____
_____
_____
_____
_____
_____
_____
_____
_____
_____
_____
_____
_____

Date:

Design a wardrobe that you'd put on to feel better immediately.

___
___
___
___
___
___
___
___
___
___
___
___
___
___
___
___

Date:

How do you think about the state of your physical condition in the present moment?

Date:

What undesirable habits should you quit doing to become more fit?

_____
_____
_____
_____
_____
_____
_____
_____
_____
_____
_____
_____
_____
_____
_____

Date:

What do you think are the three most irritating things? Make you mad?

Date:

List the things that you find frustrating most.

Date:

Send a heartfelt letter of love to someone you love dearly.

Date:

Write an acknowledgment note to the family member.

Date:

What is the most enjoyable activity you'd like to begin?

_____
_____
_____
_____
_____
_____
_____
_____
_____
_____
_____
_____
_____
_____
_____
_____

Date:

What are your favorite books? Enjoy reading that makes you feel good?

Date:

What is your ideal lifestyle appear to

Date:

Record a moment when you assisted someone in a way that felt good about you.

Date:

Create your list of friends you must stop spending time with.

_____
_____
_____
_____
_____
_____
_____
_____
_____
_____
_____
_____
_____
_____
_____

Date:

Who has the most significant influence on you?

Date:

What would be the most important thing you'll do after waking up in the early morning?

Date:

What is your most-loved self-care practice?

Date:

How do you feel about rewarding yourself when you do something positive for yourself?

_____
_____
_____
_____
_____
_____
_____
_____
_____
_____
_____
_____
_____
_____
_____

Date:

Write five things you're grateful for in your life.

_____
_____
_____
_____
_____
_____
_____
_____
_____
_____
_____
_____
_____
_____

Date:

How do you envision your life will look 10 years from today?

Date:

Write a positive affirmation that you can repeat to yourself anytime you're feeling anxious.

Date:

When was the most recent time you had an anxiety attack?

Date:

When did you last experience an uncontrollable nightmare?

Date:

How does social media affect your mood?

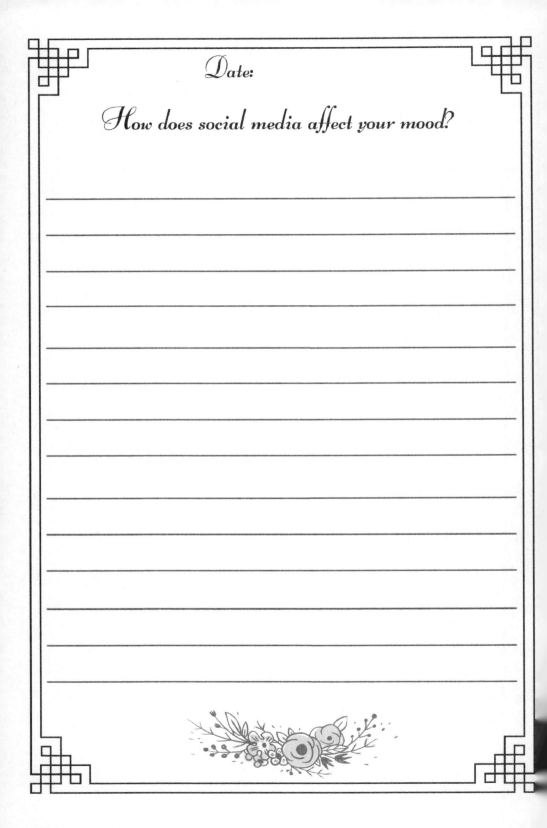

Date:

Create an inventory of the people you want to remove from the social networks you use.

Date:

Draw what you feel at the moment.

Date:

Write down all the things that keep you awake at night.

Date:

What are your most important values?

Date:

Do you love yourself? What is the reason or the reason not?

_____
_____
_____
_____
_____
_____
_____
_____
_____
_____
_____
_____
_____
_____
_____
_____

Date:

Note down any words you are running through your head at this moment.

Date:

What are the five people you would like to spend the most time with?

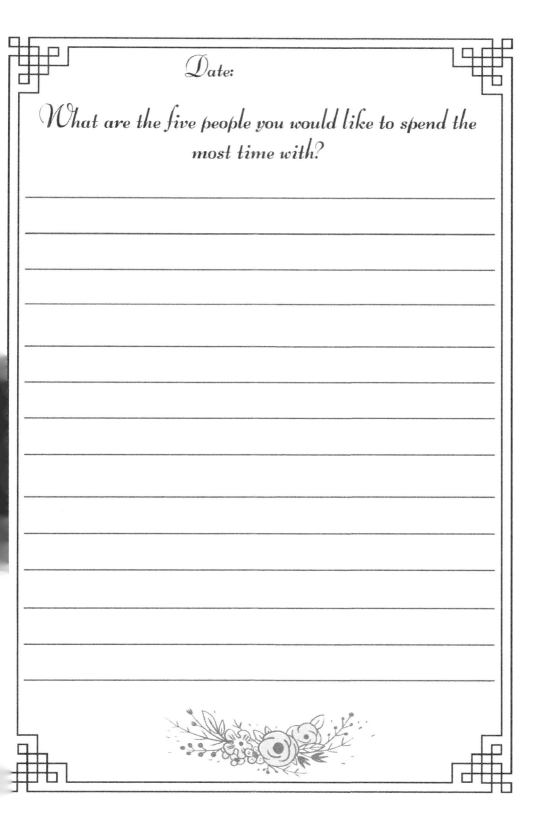

Date:

Note down the positive habits you would like to develop.

Date:

Do you have any suggestions to improve your life?

Date:

Write down the things you have experienced in life you'd like to go through.

Date:

What do you think are your current goals for the shutdown?

Date:

What do you currently have as lockdown goals?

Date:

What areas of your life aren't receiving enough attention? For example, relationships, career, fitness, et cetera.

Date:

Write an email for your next self. What do you want to include in your goals? What achievements would you have made?

Date:

How did social distancing make you feel?

Date:

If money were not a factor to your daily life?

Date:

Write down specific things that are happening very well in your life right now.

Date:

Do You have a routine for your morning?

$\mathcal{D}$ate:

$\mathcal{W}$hat are some things you enjoy doing before you go to bed at the end of the night?

Date:

Choose one thing you'd prefer to let go of and write a note to remind yourself of those issues.

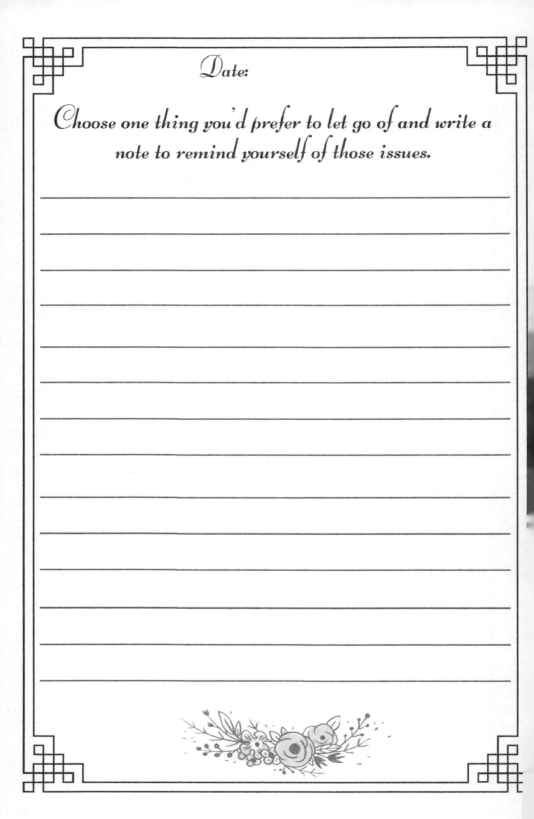

Date:

How do you deal with negative feelings?

Date:

What brings you peace?

Date:

What is the most significant moment in your life?

Date:

Write about your most fearful phobia.

Date:

From an index of 1 to 10, how tranquil do you feel now? The lowest is and the other is the most serene.

Date:

What can you do to help you conquer the anxiety you have experienced in the past?

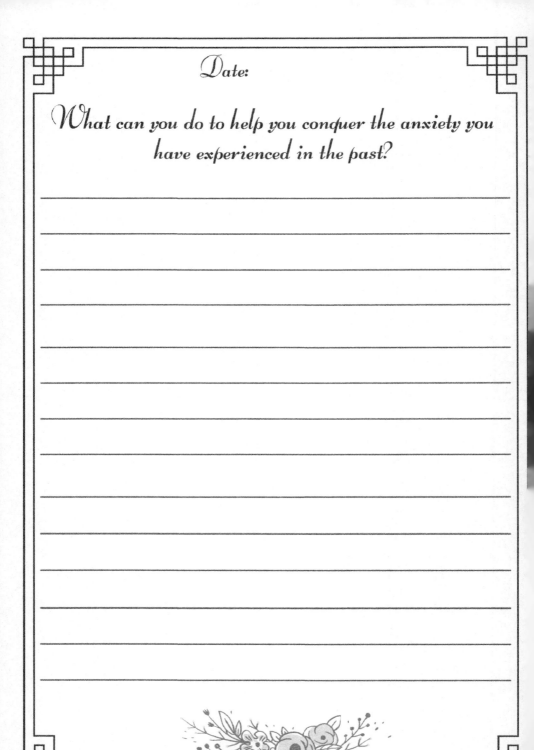

Date:

Write down your most happy memory.

Date:

Note 5 things you do that make you feel happy after a tiring day.

_____
_____
_____
_____
_____
_____
_____
_____
_____
_____
_____
_____
_____
_____
_____
_____
_____

Date:

Make a list of the things that make you satisfied daily. For instance, the Sun shining brightly, taking a long walk, binge-watching a TV show, or.

Date:

How can journaling help you?

Date:

If you could alter one aspect of your life, What would you choose to change? Make the list of prioritizations for the upcoming week.

Date:

If you could escape and hide now, which direction would you take? And why?

_____
_____
_____
_____
_____
_____
_____
_____
_____
_____
_____
_____
_____
_____
_____

Date:

Write an address to your teenager self.

Date:

What do you sleep for? Do you use your mobile during the night? Write down ten things you would like people to know about you.

_____
_____
_____
_____
_____
_____
_____
_____
_____
_____
_____
_____
_____
_____
_____
_____
_____

Date:

What tips would you offer someone who is experiencing an emotional time at the moment?

_____
_____
_____
_____
_____
_____
_____
_____
_____
_____
_____
_____
_____
_____
_____

Date:

Choose one positive phrase you'd repeat to yourself every single day as you get up in the morning.

Date:

What could you do today to feel better?

_____

_____

_____

_____

_____

_____

_____

_____

_____

_____

_____

_____

_____

_____

Date:

What are some things you're running away from at the moment?

_____
_____
_____
_____
_____
_____
_____
_____
_____
_____
_____
_____
_____
_____
_____
_____

Date:

What is it that makes you feel satisfied?

Date:

What would your ideal day appear to be?

Date:

What could you possibly live without?

Date:

In which place do you feel the most secure? What is the most important way you can increase your spirituality?

___

___

___

___

___

___

___

___

___

___

___

___

___

___

___

___

___

___

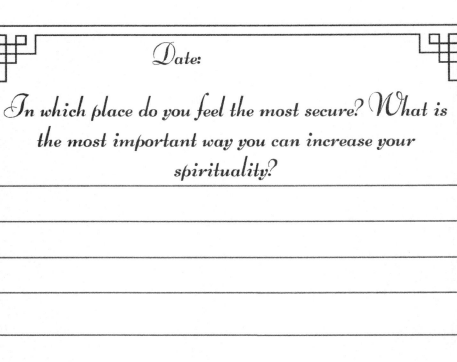

Date:

What would your ideal life be like?

Date:

Which is most significant for yourself in life?

Date:

What is your most tremendous anxiety?

Date:

If Jeannie will make three wishes for you, what wish would you want to ask for?

Date:

Create your dream life. Define it clearly.

Date:

Write about a challenging situation you have overcome through the years.

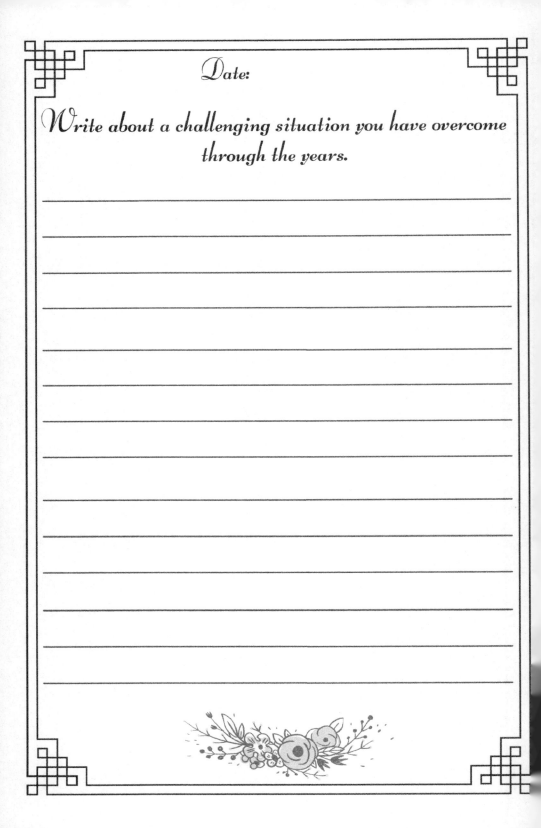

Date:

Send an email to someone who has caused you to feel anxious.

Date:

Consider a situation where you've faced setbacks, and what were you able to accomplish to overcome those setbacks?

Date:

When you think of the future, do you feel nervous or happy?

Date:

What is it that gives you strength in the most challenging moments within your own life?

_____
_____
_____
_____
_____
_____
_____
_____
_____
_____
_____
_____
_____
_____
_____
_____

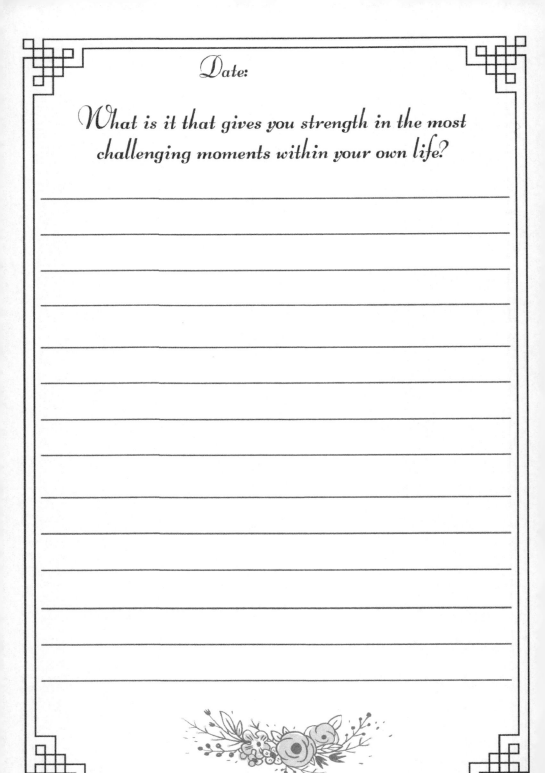

Date: _____ _____   Mon   Tue   Wed   Thu   Fri   Sat   Sun

Today I'm grateful for:

Best thing about today:

Today's positive affirmation:

Date: ___ ___   Mon   Tue   Wed   Thu   Fri   Sat   Sun

Today I'm grateful for:

Best thing about today:

Today's positive affirmation:

Date: ___ ___   Mon   Tue   Wed   Thu   Fri   Sat   Sun

Today I'm grateful for:

Best thing about today:

Today's positive affirmation:

Date: _____ _____   Mon   Tue   Wed   Thu   Fri   Sat   Sun

Today I'm grateful for:

Best thing about today:

Today's positive affirmation:

Date: _____ _____   Mon   Tue   Wed   Thu   Fri   Sat   Sun

Today I'm grateful for:

Best thing about today:

Today's positive affirmation:

Date: ___ ___   Mon   Tue   Wed   Thu   Fri   Sat   Sun

Today I'm grateful for:

Best thing about today:

Today's positive affirmation:

Date: ___ ___   Mon   Tue   Wed   Thu   Fri   Sat   Sun

Today I'm grateful for:

Best thing about today:

Today's positive affirmation:

Date: _____   Mon   Tue   Wed   Thu   Fri   Sat   Sun

Today I'm grateful for:

Best thing about today:

Today's positive affirmation:

Date: _____ _____   Mon   Tue   Wed   Thu   Fri   Sat   Sun

Today I'm grateful for:

Best thing about today:

Today's positive affirmation:

Date: ___ ___   Mon   Tue   Wed   Thu   Fri   Sat   Sun

Today I'm grateful for:

Best thing about today:

Today's positive affirmation:

Date: _____ ___   Mon   Tue   Wed   Thu   Fri   Sat   Sun

Today I'm grateful for:

Best thing about today:

Today's positive affirmation:

Date: ___ ___   Mon   Tue   Wed   Thu   Fri   Sat   Sun

Today I'm grateful for:

Best thing about today:

Today's positive affirmation:

Date: ___ ___   Mon   Tue   Wed   Thu   Fri   Sat   Sun

Today I'm grateful for:

Best thing about today:

Today's positive affirmation:

Date: ___ ___   Mon   Tue   Wed   Thu   Fri   Sat   Sun

Today I'm grateful for:

Best thing about today:

Today's positive affirmation:

Date: ___ ___   Mon   Tue   Wed   Thu   Fri   Sat   Sun

Today I'm grateful for:

Best thing about today:

Today's positive affirmation:

Date: ___ ___   Mon   Tue   Wed   Thu   Fri   Sat   Sun

Today I'm grateful for:

Best thing about today:

Today's positive affirmation:

Date: ___ ___   Mon   Tue   Wed   Thu   Fri   Sat   Sun

Today I'm grateful for:

Best thing about today:

Today's positive affirmation:

Date: ___ ___   Mon   Tue   Wed   Thu   Fri   Sat   Sun

Today I'm grateful for:

Best thing about today:

Today's positive affirmation:

Date: ___ ___ Mon Tue Wed Thu Fri Sat Sun

Today I'm grateful for:

Best thing about today:

Today's positive affirmation:

Date: ___ ___ Mon Tue Wed Thu Fri Sat Sun

Today I'm grateful for:

Best thing about today:

Today's positive affirmation: